3

RECITATIONS FOR CHURCH OCCASIONS

BY MELVIN WATERS

CONTENTS

DEDICATION

When I was a child, we used to sing a song that went, "Give me my flowers while I live, so that I can see the glory that they bring." Those days are long gone but the spirit in that song still lives on in my heart.

In remembrance of that song, I dedicate this book to my Aunt Charlotte Croom (74) of Dover, North Carolina. When most ladies her age retire and enjoy their grandchildren, Aunt Charlotte decided to start a church. She is the founding pastor of Malachi Church of God in Kinston, North Carolina. She preaches the uncompromising gospel each Sunday. When most people her age will not even get into a boat, she has stepped out of the boat, always keeping her eyes on Jesus. Even after excruciating hip surgery, she continues running for Jesus—though at a little slower gait.

At this writing, she and Uncle James just celebrated their 56th wedding anniversary. They raised six children on their farm. Their offspring still love God and their parents.

She still uses my two previous recitations books. She is a much trusted source of inspiration and wisdom to me. I take delight in dedicating this book to my sweet Aunt (Reverend) Charlotte Croom of Dover, North Carolina . . . "You go, girl!"

FOREWORD

It is not the quality of the brain that determines a man but the character of the soul.

The leadership of Pastor Melvin Waters is unchallenged. First, he trusts in God, second, he trusts in his fellowman, and third, he trusts in himself. As a very young student in school he enriched the hearts of many of his teachers and his fellow classmates. He was an ardent church worker in the youth department of the church and was devoted to the growth and activities of the church in a very creditable manner.

As a high school scholar he exemplified the ability to assume responsibility. He adhered to high standards of moral value and positive qualities of outstanding scholarship. We can best describe him as an adult as a dedicated minister, a businessman, an educator and humanitarian; a person whose life has always stressed that achievements mean nothing without love and without sharing knowledge and resources with all human beings. His is a tie of faith and spiritual unity. His is a tie of service rendered in forgetfulness of self and for the greater common good.

How proud his wife, his sons, his mother, his church members, and his friends must be as they have been the foundation, through prayers and support, for the unwavering commitment to this project. How fortunate we are to have the privilege of knowing a gentleman of such rich character as Pastor Melvin Waters.

Mrs. Nannie Ruth Loftin
Former High School English Teacher
Woodington High School
Kinston, North Carolina

PREFACE

Words can be seeds of future reality. By words, men and women can be moved to accomplish greatness. There are dozens of references in the Bible with the words, "God said . . ." in them. These words reflect the creative power of Jehovah. How about your words? Do they move people? Do they encourage people? Do they help to make a positive difference?

Well, none of us speaks as creatively as God does. However, we do have the power to speak into people's lives with positive words. I believe words spoken with grace will both bless and prosper others. I pray that the words of this book will be " . . . apples of gold in a tapestry of silver."

Pastor Mel Waters

WORDS OF APPRECIATION

PASTOR APPRECIATION

Today, we want to show our appreciation for a wonderful under-shepherd and sibling in Christ. [He/She] has served as our pastor for [number of years]. [He/She] has regularly led us to the green pastures of God's Word. As we pause to honor [name], we are ever thankful to God for blessing us with this [man/woman] of God.

● ● ●

A good pastor is hard to find; a great pastor, even harder. We are here today to show appreciation for a great pastor. What is a great pastor? Well the G stands for godly, the R stands for reverent, the E stands for edifier, the A stands for available, and the T stands for tender. Pastor [name], we honor you today for the great ways God has blessed us through you.

● ● ●

Most people do not receive words of appreciation until they are long gone. We believe one should be given their flowers while they are alive. Pastor [name] has faithfully labored in this church for [number of years]. [He/She] has established a legacy of faithfulness and godliness. We thank God for Pastor [name] and appreciate [him/her] more than [he/she] will ever know.

● ● ●

Thanks to each of you for attending our pastor's appreciation service. Your presence here shows that you too appreciate Pastor [name]. [He/She] has labored faithfully here for [number of years]. We give [him/her] our thanks for a job of excellence. Thank you very much, Pastor [name].

Today, it is our delight to dedicate this service to our pastor, [Brother/Sister] [Name]. [His/Her] faithful labor of love has blessed so many of us. We are inspired and empowered to go forth in the power of the Holy Spirit. God has so blessed us to have a leader who helps us to know God better. May the words and activity of this day honor God as we bless Pastor [Name].

Pastor [Name] has served faithfully as our under-shepherd for [number of years]. Many of us came to faith in Christ through [his/her] ministry. Others of us have been strengthened and called to ministry under [his/her] tutelage. Today, we pause to recognize Pastor [name] and to show appreciation for what God has done through [him/her]. May God smile upon these efforts to bless a truly humble [man/woman] of God.

SHORT FAMILY DEVOTIONS OF APPRECIATION

Scripture: Psalm 37:25

"I was young and now I am old, yet I have never seen the righteous forsaken or their children begging bread."

Reflections: Regardless of our age, the scene of a little child running and jumping refreshes the heart. Jesus loved little children and ministered to them in several of His meetings. Children are "a heritage from the Lord." The children of the righteous possess a blessing of ongoing provision from God.

As we look with appreciation on these children, we thank God for them and His hand of protection upon each one. As we look at the Heavenly Father, we gain strength to be better earthly parents in every sense of the word. Dear God, thank You for Your provision to us. Amen.

● ● ●

Scripture: Exodus 20:12

"Honor your father and your mother, so that you may live long in the land the LORD your God is giving you."

Reflections: This passage is one of the few commandments with a promise. God wants each child to revere his parents. When we were children, they nurtured and protected us. As we grew older, they were instruments of God's wisdom. In some sense, the way we treat them is the way we will be treated ourselves.

Grant us, O God, the ability to always honor our parents. Help us to seek Your wisdom in gaining provision for their needs. As our Heavenly Father, walk with us as we walk with them. Amen.

Scripture: Matthew 12:50

"For whoever does the will of my Father in heaven is my brother and sister and mother."

Reflections: The special relationship between believers is somewhat paradoxical. In marriage relationships, a man's wife is also his sister. No wonder the writer of Ephesians 5:21 encourages us to "submit to one another." When Jesus said the words of Matthew 12:50, the listeners were thinking on a single dimension. Jesus rightly stated who His "brother and sister and mother" really were.

Dear Lord, in our earthly relationships, help us to honor those who are our spiritual siblings. Give us a heart to truly love them so that all men will know that we are Your disciples. Amen.

● ● ●

Scripture: 1 John 4:7-8

"Dear friends, let us love one another, for love comes from God. Everyone who loves has been born of God and knows God. Whoever does not love does not know God, because God is love."

Reflections: Of all the words in our vocabulary, love is probably the most misunderstood. An old song says, "Love is not a feeling, it's an act of your will." This is so true. Each of us must see love as an active word. "You can give without loving but you cannot love without giving." God showed His love for us by giving His Son, history's greatest act of love. As children of God, we must be a reflection of God's love to believers and nonbelievers.

Dear God, please make us an instrument of Your love. Let us be "Your hands extended" and a facilitator of blessing. Thank You, Father, for Your love and the ability to love in a healthy way. Amen.

SINGLE PARENTS RECOGNITION

(Ask single parents to stand.) For various reasons, many parents raise children by themselves. It is the place of the church to show God's love and help to these brave men and women. Today we recognize the tireless efforts of single parents who sacrifice and work so their children can have a better life. We honor them and pray God's blessings upon them for strength and wisdom as they stand and are recognized.

● ● ●

Dear God, being a single parent is one of life's most difficult ministries. However, we see in Your Word in Philippians 4:13 that, "I can do everything through him who gives me strength." Give each of our single parents strength and wisdom to raise mighty men and women of God. Help us to stand with them in prayer as they honor You in their efforts. Amen.

● ● ●

"One is a lonely number," especially when you are raising children by yourself. The mere presence of single parents here today shows that God is the silent partner in their lives. May God's grace and love empower each single parent to raise their children in the ways of God. Bless them now as we honor them in Jesus' name. Amen.

● ● ●

As single parents increase in society, so should our resolve increase to pray for them. They need not only our prayers but our encouragement and practical help in raising their children. May God give them wisdom and stamina to successfully raise the next generation. Help each of us to remember them and to help them in their ministry to their family. Amen.

Single and lonely
But not alone
For my silent partner
Sits on heaven's throne.
Pray for me daily
As I walk down life's mile
To gently guide and shepherd
The gift of God—my child.

SPEAKER APPRECIATION COMMENTS

What a wonderful address. Our hearts were touched by your inspiring words. May we now apply the tenets of this speech as we go from this place.

● ● ●

We thank God for such a superb speech. I pray that these words will be the seeds of greater accomplishments in each of us. Again, let's applaud our speaker.

● ● ●

Such wonderful comments are destined for the speaker's hall of fame. However, may these words become reality in our lives as a fitting tribute to this speaker.

● ● ●

We thank God that we heard from Him through our speaker. May the fruit of these words resonate and become visible in all of our lives. Again, we thank God's messenger for the message.

● ● ●

Our speaker has delivered heaven's mail today. May the words of [his/her] message empower each of us to walk out its principles. May we bless others as a result of the blessing we have received.

May the words we received today make us all better persons. May we take this message and walk as a "living epistle" read by all men. [Name], we thank you for breaking and distributing the "bread of life" to each of us. May God continue to use you to bring men to Him.

Our hearts were "strangely warmed" as we listened to these words. May each of us commit to be the hands and feet of what we heard. Bless now our speaker, dear Lord, as [he/she] continues to be a carrier of Your Word.

We hear many speeches with our ears; but today, we heard with our hearts. May the message of this speaker capture us and help us to be vessels of freedom for others. Let's again give our speaker a hand!

Words without anointing are mere empty phrases. They mean little and bore us a lot. However, we have just heard from the throne room of heaven. Our lives can never be the same. Dear Lord, empower us to obey what we heard and to bless others with its admonition.

Thank you, Father God, for what we have heard. Bless the messenger of Your Word. May [he/she] continue to be an instrument of your empowering grace.

SUNDAY SCHOOL TEACHER APPRECIATION

People rarely know their names. They spend countless hours teaching our children God's Word. But our Sunday School teachers are the world's best and we thank them today for their wonderful devotion to God and to our children.

● ● ●

Today we want everyone to know how much we appreciate our Sunday School teachers. Their tireless devotion to teaching God's Word to our precious children is greatly appreciated. May God continue to richly bless them and again . . . thanks!

● ● ●

What a joyful occasion it is for us to publicly thank our Sunday School teachers. They minister to the most precious members of our church. May God bless them as they teach the children of this church.

● ● ●

Jesus said in Luke 18:16, "Let the little children come to me, and do not hinder them, for the kingdom of God belongs to such as these." Our Sunday School teachers help bring our children to Jesus. For their wonderful work, we give them a hearty "thank you!"

WORDS OF DEDICATION

BUSINESS DEDICATION

Lord, we thank You for giving us wisdom to develop this business. Help us to bless our customers with excellent products and services. May we first listen to You as we work to meet their needs. We commit to serve our customers by serving You in Jesus' name. Amen.

● ● ●

Dear God, may we rightly invest the talents You have given us. This business is Yours and we want to work with You in blessing others. Let each worker be aware that Christ is the executive officer in this venture. Help us to pray daily for better ways to serve our clientele. Thank You for allowing us to be a blessing to You by blessing others. Amen.

● ● ●

Almighty Father, You give ideas and wisdom for "witty inventions." We invite Your presence and wisdom as we embark upon this business venture. Help us to listen attentively and to meet the needs of our customers. Be with us as we minister in the business arena as an agent of the kingdom of God. Please bless now the work of our hands in Jesus' name. Amen.

● ● ●

Lord God, first we thank You for this wonderful business opportunity. Your wisdom and guidance has made this day possible. Walk with us as we minister in the marketplace. Make us constant companions of excellence in daily service. We thank You in advance for Your guidance and favor upon this business. Amen.

Father God, we commit this business to You. Your hand led us to launch out into this venture. Your wisdom helped make this day a reality. Now we ask for continued wisdom and guidance as we endeavor to honor You in all we do. May we constantly call upon You as our CEO and may our customer service be a picture of compassionate grace. Please walk with us and bless us now in Jesus' name. Amen.

● ● ●

Our business is Your business, dear God. We want to honor You in all we do. Help us to serve our customers with excellence and grace. Grant to us the will to daily project the attitude of the carpenter's Son. May we constantly call upon the Holy Spirit of God for direction and wisdom. May every customer see a picture of Jesus in the way we interact with him or her. Use us now as an instrument of Your Son in the marketplace. We pray in Jesus' name, Amen.

CHURCH MOTHERS DEDICATION SERVICE

Dear Lord, words cannot express our appreciation for the mothers of this church. They have labored hard in prayer and in practical ways on behalf of our church. Today we dedicate this service to them. May they be continually strengthened in their walk with You as they help the people of this church. Amen.

● ● ●

Father God, we are so blessed to have these church mothers in our congregation. Their diligent service over the years has greatly helped our church. Their love for God is ever-present and evident in our midst. We dedicate this service to them as we "give honor to whom honor is due." Bless them as they receive our appreciation today. Amen.

● ● ●

Today we are delighted to honor the mothers of this church. All of us have been blessed by their ministry to this portion of Christ's body. Much of their labor is known only in heaven because of their humility.

As we honor them, may they understand just how much we love and appreciate them. Bless them now, dear God, in Jesus' name. Amen.

● ● ●

The mothers of our church are foundation pillars in this body. Their love for God is the source of their strength. They encourage the old and mentor the young in their spiritual journeys. We love them and dedicate this service to them in Jesus' name. Amen.

This service is dedicated to the stalwart mothers of our church. Their love for God and ministry to our church is a thing of beauty. As we bestow honor on them today, we are most thankful to God for His gift to our church. These ladies are highly esteemed in our midst and the object of this appreciation service. May God continue to use them and to bless many through their ministries. Amen.

God has blessed us with the mothers of our church. Their untiring efforts challenge us all to be more like Jesus. The Lord has blessed us with them. Today we pause to recognize them as pillars of our church. We dedicate this service to them for their love and service to God and to us.

CHURCH VEHICLES

Father God, we thank You for the resources to get these vehicles. We pray a blessing of safety over each of them. May Your angels guide the drivers as they transport people to church and back. We dedicate these vehicles to God's service in Jesus' name. Amen.

Dear Lord, our desire is to win souls into the kingdom of God. In order to do that, we have obtained these vehicles to bring people to hear God's word. May each vehicle travel in safety and peace with their precious human cargo. In the name of Jesus, we now dedicate these vehicles to be used for godly purposes and kingdom pursuits. Amen.

Father God, You have blessed us with these wonderful vehicles. From the storeroom of heaven, we have gotten resources to minister to the lost and the found. We pray a blessing of safety over each driver and vehicle. We also pray that everyone riding on these vehicles will hear and respond to the message of the gospel. In Jesus' name, we now dedicate these vehicles to the ministry of the gospel. Amen.

Dear God, as these vehicles travel the streets and highways, may they be a reminder of Your love and grace. May each driver be a living epistle of Jesus. Please keep each vehicle safe as they carry valuable lives to places of ministry. In Your authority, we now dedicate each vehicle to the gospel ministry. Amen.

As these vehicles travel the highways of this city, may they be safe from harm and danger. The passengers in each vehicle are people for whom Christ died. We are so appreciative to God for blessing us with these conveyances. We dedicate these vehicles to the glory and use of God in helping others to go to church and other community activities. Amen.

NEW BABY

The psalmist wrote in Psalm 127 that, "Children are a gift from the Lord." Heavenly Father, we thank You for this precious gift. May this child's life honor and glorify Your name. We pray the blessings of the Lord on this child from the top of [his/her] head to the soles of [his/her] feet.

● ● ●

May [his/her] mind constantly meditate upon God's Word. (Psalms 119:15)

May [his/her] eyes constantly behold blessings from the Lord. (Matthew 13:16)

May God's Word always be hidden in [his/her] heart. (Psalm 119:11)

May [his/her] hands always do the work of God. (Proverbs 12:24)

May [his/her] arms be strong as [he/she] helps to bear others' burdens. (Galatians 6:2)

May [his/her] body always be a healthy temple of the Holy Spirit. (1 Corinthians 6:19)

May [his/her] legs run swiftly with the gospel of peace. (Ephesians 6:15)

May [his/her] feet reflect Your beauty as a carrier of good news. (Romans 10:15)

● ● ●

Father, we pray that You will bless [his/her] parents with a strong healthy marriage. May they always depend upon You for wisdom as they raise this mighty servant of God. We pray a special blessing upon [his/her] siblings. May this baby grow up in a healthy family environment of acceptance, grace, and love. As a church body, please remind us to pray for this family. Father, we now sanctify (set apart) and dedicate this baby for the work of the gospel in Jesus' name. Amen.

NEW HYMNALS

O God, we thank You for these new hymnals. Their words speak of Your love and grace. We dedicate them to You as instruments of worship and praise. May each singer and listener be drawn to the realization of Your love and eternal salvation. Amen.

These hymnals point to the eternal Savior who is worthy to be praised and worshiped. The words on each page move our hearts to a place of contemplation and meditation. On this wonderful day, we humbly dedicate them to the service of God. While human toil paid the tangible price of each book, we revel in the fact that Jesus' blood paid an even bigger price for our salvation. May each singer come to that realization, we pray in Jesus' name. Amen.

While these books alone hold no special power, the Person spoken of in each song is most special. These books speak of the hand of God moving among mankind. As we dedicate these books to the service of God, may each person using these books come to the knowledge of God's salvation. We pronounce a blessing upon those who will sing the songs of Zion recorded upon these pages. Amen.

Dear God, we dedicate these new hymnals for use in facilitating worship and praise to You. May each user be "strangely warmed" by the Spirit of God as they look upon the pages. May God's Word come alive in their hearts as kingdom music brings joy to each heart. Thank You, Lord, for those who labored to give us these hymnals and bless them now in Jesus' name. Amen.

Almighty God, first we thank You for Jesus of whom these pages constantly speak. Next, we thank You for the faithful servants who worked for the resources to provide these hymnals. We dedicate each book to You, Father God, in the hope and belief that the user of each book will come to know You. Bless us now as we bless You in the use of these earthly tomes for kingdom purposes. Amen.

Pew Bibles

Heavenly Father, may these Bibles be used to help strengthen believers and to help evangelize those outside the faith. In these books, the heart of God is revealed to the hearts of men. By these books many lives have been transformed by the Spirit of God. We now dedicate them to kingdom use in Jesus' name. Amen.

● ● ●

The words in these Bibles mean little without the changing power of God's Spirit. No other book in history has impacted mankind as much as the Bible. Words from these books have been the turning point of many of our lives. Our desire is that these Bibles continue their transforming work in the hearts of men. We dedicate them to God's service in Jesus' name. Amen.

● ● ●

The word "Bible" means "book of books." These books present God's means of salvation for humanity. They have stood strong against the tides of criticism. These books, though new in appearance, still resonate with the voice of "The Ancient of Days." With great delight and expectation we dedicate these Bibles for kingdom use.

● ● ●

We dedicate these Bibles to God's purpose in the earth. He wills that all come to "the knowledge of the truth." May each reader come to "know God and to make Him known." May the blessings of reading the Word resound throughout the lives of each reader. May every ear listen to God through His Word and obey Him by the Spirit's power. Almighty God, be honored in the years to come by our dedication of these Bibles into Your service. Amen.

The children's song goes, "My B-I-B-L-E, now that's the book for me; I stand upon the word of God, my B-I-B-L-E!" These words, though written for a child, express the reality of the Bible. As we dedicate these Bibles, we pray a blessing upon everyone who reads them from this day forward. May God's Word take root in every reader's heart and facilitate eternal change in their life. Thank You, dear Lord, for Your Word and for the opportunity to make it known to others. Amen.

WORDS OF INTRODUCTION

NEW CHURCH OFFICERS

What a pleasure it is for me to introduce to you our new [church position]. [Name] has been a member of this body for [number of years]. We are delighted that God has placed [him/her] in this position and look forward to working with [him/her] in [his/her] new capacity. Let's all give a hand to [name].

● ● ●

[Name] has graciously consented to serve as [church position]. He has served as [previous positions] and is the spouse of [spouse's name] and [father/mother] of [children's names]. Let's pray for [him/her] as [he/she] begins serving God in this new position.

● ● ●

The office of [position] is a very important position in our church. We have labored in prayer for God's choice for this position. We believe we have God's choice for this office. We are happy to have [name] agree to serve as [position].

● ● ●

God has answered our prayers for the person to serve as [position]. This person has served as [past positions] and is a contributing member to this church. [He/She] knows God and loves God with all [his/her] heart. With great delight, I present to you our new [position].

Our church is truly blessed to have great men and women of God. Over the past months, we have prayed for someone to fill the position of [office]. We believe we have received God's choice for this new position. Please join with me as we welcome our new [position], [name of person].

One of life's greatest privileges is to serve God by serving others. In the church, there are many opportunities to be of service. Today we are excited to name the next [position] of our church. [He/She] has served faithfully and is now taking on a new responsibility. Let's give a hand to [name], our new [position].

Serving God is one of life's greatest joys. In our church, we are blessed to have wonderful servants of the Lord. When we needed a [position], we went to prayer for the right person to fill the vacancy. We believe God answered our prayers by giving us [name] to fill the position. Please give a hearty "praise the Lord" as we recognize [name], our new [position].

VISITING MINISTER

What a pleasure it is for us to have [name of minister] from [name of his/her church] with us today. [He/She] is a graduate of [name of school] and has served as [past pastorates and jobs].

However, [his/her] greatest claim to fame is that [he/she] is the spouse of [spouse's name] and the parent of [names of children].

Please join me in welcoming [name of pastor].

● ● ●

Our speaker today is a dear friend of this church. [He/She] is the spouse of [spouse's name] and the parent of [children's names]. [He/She] serves as [title] and is a graduate of [name of schools].

Let's give a hearty welcome to [name of speaker].

● ● ●

[Name of speaker] is a wonderful friend and competent minister of the gospel. [He/She] serves as [title] at [name of church]. [He/She] has written [number of books] and is a much requested speaker.

However, next to knowing Jesus, [he/she] is the spouse of [name of spouse] and the parent of [children's names and ages].

Ladies and gentlemen, let us give a hearty [name of church] welcome to [name of speaker].

● ● ●

God has blessed us today to have [name of speaker] as our guest speaker. [He/She] is the spouse of [name of spouse] and the parent of [names of children]. [He/She] loves God with all [his/her] heart and expresses that love as [title] of [name of church]. Let us prepare our hearts to receive God's Word from our speaker, [name of speaker].

Today's speaker is an honorable and respected [man/woman] of God. [He/She] is also the spouse of [spouse's name] and the parent of [names of children]. [He/She] serves as [title] of [name of church] and is a graduate of [names of schools]. [He/She] has written [names of books] and is a much requested speaker.

Let us welcome [name of speaker].

VISITORS

(Ask visitors to stand to recognize them.) What a delight to have each of you with us today. May God richly bless you as you share with us in this worship experience. Please remain standing as the ushers present you with a token of our appreciation for your presence.

Thank you so much for visiting with us today. May God minister to you as you partake with us in worship and the Word. From this day forward, consider yourself a member of this family.

On behalf of the pastor and staff of this church, we thank you for visiting with us today. May God richly bless you as you worship with us and enjoy God's presence. We invite you to come join with us as we serve God and evangelize our world.

What a delight to have you with us! We love to fellowship with the children of God. Even though you are a visitor today, you are welcome to join with us as we make the Savior known to the world. Again, welcome!

Welcome friends and loved-ones.
We are glad to have you here.
Relax and join in worship for Christ the Lord is near.

Be blessed and make Him welcome.
He loves to hear your praise.
Again be welcome with us. His banner proudly raise.

We're glad to have you with us
     As we enjoy God's grace
For He is Lord and Master,
     And Messiah in this place.
Sit down or stand and worship,
     And join in praise and prayer
For from this day and onward
     Enjoy the Savior's care.

REPLIES TO INTRODUCTIONS

Thank you for that wonderful introduction. I am humbled by it and encouraged to do my best to live up to it. Again, thank you.

● ● ●

Such an introduction may have gotten more applause than what I have to say. I'd better get going and make it true. Thank you for your warm welcome!

● ● ●

Wow! What an introduction! I surely hope what follows will be just as good. Thank you for such a warm introduction.

● ● ●

May the words that follow befit the words of this gracious preamble. I offer my humblest appreciation for your kind words.

● ● ●

This is the best introduction I have ever received. I hope that you can say the same of what is to follow.

● ● ●

I am both humbled and inspired by this introduction. Thank you for such kind comments. Now, let me see if I am equal to this introduction.

● ● ●

May the Lord richly repay you for that wonderful introduction. I also hope He will make me worthy of it as I speak.

Thank you for those kind words. Pray for me as I speak words that I hope will bless each hearer.

I think I will get a recording of that introduction. It was inspiring and hopefully empowering as I begin this address.

God is truly good to this speaker. That wonderful introduction was kindness personified. I pray that I will speak words of humility encased in grace.

That introduction will be laminated in my mind. I plan to get an audio copy of it and I will play it when I am feeling down. Now, though, I hope I can reply with words that will be just as encouraging.

PRAYERS AND BLESSINGS

CHRISTMAS PRAYERS

Dear Lord, thank You for sending the Prince of Peace. May the splendor of this season shine brightly in all of our hearts. Bestow to each of us the power to love others with God's love. May the Baby in the manger reign supremely in each of our lives. Amen.

● ● ●

Heavenly Father, You showed Your love for us by sending Jesus. During this season, we affirm our desire to show Your love to others. From the gift in the Bethlehem stable to gifts under our trees, may the spirit of giving resound in the heart of mankind. Thank You for loving us and using us as vehicles of grace. Amen.

● ● ●

Dear God, as we gather here, give us a fresh anointing of love and grace. May the Christmas spirit forever remain in our hearts. May gifts seen and unseen empower us to tell the story of the Christ child in our lifestyle and in daily deeds. We love You and thank You for loving us. We pray these blessings now in the name of Jesus. Amen.

● ● ●

God Jehovah, You have "placed eternity in our hearts." Grant us during this season of giving the desire to be a blessing to others. Your love is so amazing and bountiful that You sent Jesus on our behalf. May our lives forever show gratitude for the salvation He brings. Grant us now the power to bless You by blessing others through the enablement of Your Spirit. These things we pray in Jesus' name. Amen.

We love You, Lord. We thank You for Your love for us shown by the gift of Jesus' birth in Bethlehem. His birth brought us the hope of salvation. Our gifts are a picture of the ultimate gift of heaven. May Your love be seen and accepted by all who recognize Your purpose. Bless us now in Jesus' name as we rejoice in the coming of the Prince of Peace. Amen.

Amidst the glitz and hustle of the season, dear Lord, please help us to focus on the "reason for the season." We rejoice that "Jesus is the reason for the season." Help us to show His love to everyone we know. Give us a desire to walk daily by the power of His grace. Thank You for allowing us to be a part of Your plan for our lives. Amen.

EASTER PRAYERS

Thank You, God, for Jesus' sacrifice on the cross. I, by faith, received Him as Savior and my life has never been the same. Help me to show His love to all the people I know. Bless us on this Easter Day to help heaven's population increase as others come to know Jesus too. Amen.

Heavenly Father, the gift of Your Son gave me eternal life. May the activities of this Easter Day be a fitting tribute of appreciation. Be with us as we sing, worship, and praise the Lord of Glory. Give each of us a deeper desire "to know Him and to make Him known." Thank You for Your love. In Jesus' name. Amen.

Dear Jesus, thank You for dying on the cross for us. Today we celebrate Your death and resurrection. May our words and deeds be a pleasing honor to You. Help us to show Your love to all we meet and to introduce them to You. Thank You again for all You did and all You continue to do in our lives. Amen.

Dear God, on this Easter Day our hearts are filled with appreciation, adoration, and praise for You. The three crosses on Calvary's hill all pointed towards heaven, but only Jesus' death and resurrection enabled us to know You. Because we have faith in Him, we will one day join You and Jesus in heaven. Until then, please receive today's tribute of appreciation from each of us in Jesus' name. Amen.

Heavenly Father, on this wonderful day of celebration, we rejoice in the risen Savior. By our faith, we received Him and walk in the victory of the cross. Help us to spread the word that "He is Risen!" Give us Your plan for each of our lives as we honor Jesus on this Easter Day. Amen.

The cry goes out that "He is Risen!" Our hearts rejoice in His victory on the cross. On this Easter Day, we remember God's grace shown to us through Jesus, the Risen Christ. Help us today to honor His sacrifice on the cross in all that we say and do. Amen.

HOME DEDICATION PRAYERS

Dear Lord, on behalf of [tenants], we thank You for this wonderful home. We realize that it takes a family to make a house a home. [Tenants] love You and invite Your abiding presence in this place. May this be a shelter from life's storms and a station of refreshing for [tenants]. Thank You again in Jesus' name. Amen.

● ● ●

Father, You delight in blessing Your children. On the occasion of [tenants] moving into this place, we thank You for blessing them. May Your angels spiritually and physically protect them. Please give them grace as they repose and prepare for the challenges of life. Thank You, Lord, for protecting everyone that lives here. Amen.

FATHER'S DAY PRAYERS

On this Father's Day, bless, dear Lord, the men in our lives who showed us a picture of You. Their labor and sacrifice contributed immeasurably to the person we see in the mirror. May the words and activities of this service be a fitting tribute to the men we are proud to call "Father." Bless now this day of reflection in Jesus' name. Amen.

● ● ●

Dear God, many of us came to know You because of the love of our fathers. On this day, help us to show our appreciation to our earthly fathers. May Your love empower each of us to so honor these men that they and You will be pleased. Thank You for our earthly fathers, dear Heavenly Father. Amen.

● ● ●

Heavenly Father, You bless us with an earthly father. On this Father's Day, help us to first remember Your love for all of us and to show Your love to our earthly fathers. We thank You that these men labored hard and taught us the lessons of life and the way to the Savior. Grant us grace as we celebrate this wonderful Father's Day. Amen.

● ● ●

The love of a father was first shown in Bethlehem when Jesus lay helpless in a manger. On this Father's Day, we first pause to thank You, God, for sending Your Son. As sons and daughters of earthly fathers, we also thank You for the wonderful men we honor here today. May their love for their family be an example for all of us to follow. Dear God, please give us grace to bestow an appropriate appreciation upon these men on this Father's Day. Amen.

Abba, Daddy, Papa—
    These words describe the man
Who loved and took care of us
    And showed us God's great plan.
His smile, his gentle manner
    Upheld us in our life.
The man who squeezed our tiny hand
    And cared for Mom, his wife.
And now we bow to honor
    With words that none can say,
Thanks Abba, Daddy, Papa.
    Enjoy this Father's Day.

● ● ●

Well, Dad,
    This is your day.
If I had all the world's money
    I would not be able to pay,
For your loving deeds are priceless
    And words cannot explain
Just how much I love you
    For working through life's pain.
So sit back, relax and do enjoy
    As we honor you "The Man,"
And feel the love we have for you
    As only Jesus can understand.

MOTHER'S DAY PRAYERS

Dear Lord, thanks for every mother gathered in this place today. We celebrate their love and sacrifice for us. Help us to show Your love to them as we remember all they have done for us. Please bless the events of this day in Jesus' name. Amen.

● ● ●

Almighty God, any woman may give birth to a child but a mother is a true blessing from God. Today we join our hearts and voices in showing our mothers how much we love them. Mother's Day is a time to recall memories of "our favorite girl" and to reflect upon our first earthly caregiver. May our reflections honor You as we honor them in Jesus' name. Amen.

● ● ●

They were the first ones to hold our hands and teach us the way to God. Obviously, I am talking about our mothers. On this Mother's Day, we remember the blessings of God through the "first lady" of our lives. Help us, dear Lord, to show our appreciation for these wonderful ladies as we celebrate Mother's Day. Amen.

● ● ●

Mother's Day is like no other holiday because of the closeness of the one we call "Mother." She was the vessel of our entry onto planet earth. In many cases, she was our first teacher, confidant, and witness of the Savior. No tangible treasure can pay her what she is worth. No amount of extravagant speeches can truly express our appreciation. Yet on this Mother's Day, we beseech You, Lord, to grant us grace to show our love and appreciation to these wonderful ladies we call "Mother." Bless us now as we honor them in Jesus' name. Amen.

Mere words of man
Cannot express
The many ways
She helps to bless.
Yet at this time
We pause to say
Thank God for her
This Mother's Day.

A picture of beauty
Adorned in a dress,
A helpmeet for Dad,
Mere words cannot express.
A shoulder to cry on,
Emboldened with a smile.
A person to rely on
Who goes the extra mile.
Often overworked
And closer than a brother,
Bless us, dear Lord, today
As we celebrate our mother.

PRAYERS FOR PERSONS ENTERING THE MILITARY

Dear God, as [name] enters the military, we pray Psalm 91 protection over [his/her] every move. May Your Spirit lead and guide [his/her] every step. May [he/she] serve this nation with faithful wisdom. Bless [him/her] now and grant [him/her] safety until [his/her] return home. Amen.

● ● ●

Almighty Father, the military is a place of rigorous training and perilous duty. As [name] enters the service, please lead and protect [him/her]. I pray [he/she] will serve well and return when [his/her] tour of duty is successfully completed. Thank You, Lord, for Your blessings. In Jesus' name, Amen!

● ● ●

Lord God, the military service is a demanding and dangerous place of duty. Please give [name] the stamina to endure the rigors of military life. May Your hand guide and protect [name] as [he/she] serves our nation. Please bring [him/her] home when [his/her] tour of duty is completed. Amen.

PATRIOTIC PRAYERS

America has been greatly blessed of God. Each year, thousands come here for a fresh start in life. We rejoice in a land where we can worship in any way we choose. We also rejoice that any citizen can rise to his God-given potential. Let us be grateful for the freedoms and privileges we enjoy as American citizens.

"God Bless America!" These words bring joy to the hearts of all who love this great nation. Even with its problems, it remains a land of bountiful opportunity. On this day of remembrance, let us be thankful for the blessings of this land that we love.

The scriptures declare, "Blessed is the nation whose God is the Lord!" (Psalm 33:12). America is a nation that recognizes and reveres God. On this patriotic occasion, we reflect upon the blessings of God and look forward with hope. Join us now as we celebrate the greatness of America.

We are delighted that each of you could join us today. Your presence represents a people who genuinely honor God and love this nation. Come with us now as we remember the blessings and look forward to even better days. "America . . . land that I love."

TRAVELING PRAYERS

Dear Lord,

Thank You for Your traveling graces on us. Thanks for the resources to come on this trip. Please sanctify or set aside our lodging area for Your purpose. Please grant us a time of reflection, recreation, and repose. Amen.

Heavenly Father,

Jesus took time to get away from the crowds. We too are taking a sabbatical for relaxation and reflection. Please help us to honor You in this time of recreation. May Your angels watch over our places of lodging and go with us as we play.

Help us to relax as Jesus did. Amen.

Father God,

We honor You in our daily work. You have given us favor and grace. Now, we take time to get away for some rest and relaxation. May Your Spirit grace us and give us peace during this time of fun and recreation.

Help us to replenish our bodies and spirits before we return.

We thank You and honor You for this time of repose. In Jesus' name. Amen!

Heavenly Father, we thank You for this opportunity to rest and relax. May our minds be refreshed as our bodies take some time off. Grant us the ability to shut off our cell phones and stay away from e-mail traffic. Bless our place of rest and protect us as we prepare to better serve You in the days to come. Amen.

Almighty God, vacations are a time to get away and recall the blessings of God. We thank You for a good vacation. As we have honored You in work, may we also honor You during this time of rest. Grant us grace and mercy as we recall the great things You have done.

We thank You for this time and commit ourselves to You afresh. Amen.

RETREAT INVOCATIONS

With great delight, we welcome each of you to this [name] retreat. In a sense, it is an advance of the kingdom of God. Let's pray and commit this time to the Lord.

Dear God, thank You for each of the attendees. May they hear a clear word from You and walk in enhanced spiritual vibrancy. Bless now the staff members and all those who have labored and will facilitate this retreat. We thank You in advance, Holy Spirit, for Your ministry to us in Jesus' name. Amen.

● ● ●

Your presence here says that you want to grow in the life of God. We are excited about what God wants to do in all of our lives. We look forward to great things from God. Let's pray!

Almighty God, please help each of us to know You better. Please keep us safe as we participate in recreational activities. Help us to give to others and to receive blessings from You. With great joy, we commit our time of ministry to You in Jesus' name. Amen.

● ● ●

On behalf of [church name], we welcome each of you to this retreat. We hope this will be a time of growth and spiritual enhancement in your lives. God's bountiful grace is here to bless each of us. Let us go before the throne of grace.

Father, thank You for safely bringing all of us here. May each of us receive from Your Spirit as we drink deeply from Your Word. May we be more empowered to be better examples of Your love. Please bless now the activities of this retreat in Jesus' name. Amen.

What a joy to have each of you here. We expect great things from God. The staff has prepared a variety of activities for your spiritual and recreational growth. Let's play hard and safe. Let us pray and get started.

Dear God, thank You for loving us and bringing us here. Speak to us by Your Spirit and empower us to better love You and others. We love You, Father, and commit this retreat to Your service. Amen.

MARITAL BLESSINGS

Dear God, please bless [name of couple] as they begin the covenant walk of marriage. Help them to daily rely upon You for wisdom and strength. Bless the fruit of their union. May their children "be blessed of the Lord." Grant them grace to honor You in their marriage in Jesus' name. Amen.

Heavenly Father, thank You for the covenant of marriage. Please bless [name of couple] as they walk together in marriage with You. Help them to love one another with Your love. Bless their children and grant them continual grace in Jesus' name. Amen.

Dear God, please bless [name of couple] as they begin their lives as husband and wife. May they reflect a picture of Christ and the church in all they do. May their children always walk with You. Please "establish their footsteps in Your Word" in Jesus' name. Amen.

Father God, thank You for the institution of marriage. Into that wonderful covenant [name of couple] join themselves today. May they always rely upon You to guide their lives. May their children come to know You early in life and always walk with You. Bless and keep them joyful in You, in Jesus' name. Amen.

Dear Lord, we bless [name of couple] as they join together in Holy Matrimony. May their covenant walk always honor You. May their children be strong in God and ever faithful. Bless now this wonderful couple and their sacred union in Jesus' name. Amen.

● ● ●

Almighty Father, thank You for the marriage covenant. May [name of couple] walk in graceful bliss as they spend their lives together. May they always be faithful to You and to one another. Give them children that will honor You and them. Bless the work of their hands now in Jesus' name. Amen.

● ● ●

Dear Lord, I now pronounce a marital blessing upon [name of couple]. Grant them favor and grace by Your Spirit's power. May their children be blessed and be a blessing. Thank You for them and their love for You and for one another. Amen.

MEAL GRACES/BLESSINGS

Dear God, thank You for the bounty of Your blessings. May this physical food empower us to do Your will. Bless now the hands that prepared this meal and help us to remember You in our fellowship today. Again, thank You, Lord, in Jesus' name. Amen.

● ● ●

Dear Lord, You are our provider. We thank You for this meal and the hands that prepared it. May we be ever mindful of Your love as we reflect upon Your provision in our lives. May this meal give us the strength to be a walking epistle "seen and read of all men." Bless now our food and fellowship in Jesus' name. Amen.

● ● ●

Father God, we look expectantly to the Lamb's Supper in heaven. Yet today, we thank You for this wonderful meal on earth. May our conversation honor You as we share in spiritual fellowship. Thank You for the preparers of this food and the relationships You provide to each of us. We love You, Lord, and all You do for us. Amen.

● ● ●

Almighty God, thank You that Jesus is the "Bread of Life." As we partake of this earthly bread, help us to remember that You are our provider. Bless each person present and help us to honor You in our conversation. Thank You for all You will do through us with the energy we will receive from this meal. In Jesus' name, Amen.

Heavenly Provider, thank You for this food and the hands that prepared it. May we honor You as we fellowship around this table. We love You, Lord, and again thank You for Your provision. Amen.

● ● ●

Dear God, we as Your children come together in thanks for Your provision. Bless us now as we bless You. Grant us now Your grace as we partake of earthly blessings. Amen.

APPEALS FOR THE NEEDY

The Bible says in Proverbs 19:17 that, "He who is kind to the poor lends to the Lord, and he will reward him for what he has done." On behalf of those who need a hand instead of a handout, we ask for your help. As you give through prayer, service, and finances we pray that God will return to you many fold. Thanks for your help.

● ● ●

Any of us could be in a place of great need without God's help. Today we ask for your help to "the least of these." Thank you for "lending to the Lord." May God reward you for your benevolence to these wonderful people.

● ● ●

Today, we are asking you to help those who cannot help themselves. We will always have the needy with us. Your gifts will enable them to help themselves and to one day give to others. May God bless you as you bless them.

● ● ●

Luke 6:38 exhorts us to "Give, and it will be given to you. A good measure, pressed down, shaken together and running over, will be poured into your lap. For with the measure you use, it will be measured to you." We are asking for help on behalf of those who need help. As you give, we pray God's blessings upon you for your benevolence.

● ● ●

As we prepare to give, we pray God's best to each of you. Your desire to help others is a wonderful picture of Christ's love. The poor give us an opportunity to be an instrument of God's grace. May you receive many times more in return for your kindness to people in need.

BLACK HISTORY
MONTH
CELEBRATION

Black history is a subset of American history. Each of us is tied to a nation which offers opportunity for those willing to apply themselves. Black History Month is a time to reflect upon the toils of a people whom God has greatly blessed. May the activities of this month honor our nation as well as the people of color who love it so much.

We are gathered here today to celebrate what God has done for the black people of America. Through much prayer and hard work, God has smiled upon us and given us many opportunities. We still have far to go but we are thankful for progress achieved. We commit this celebration to the God of our fathers in the hope of a brighter future.

Black History Month is a time of reflection and projection. We reflect upon the achievements of our past and the gleam of a bright future. The hope we have is not in ourselves but in Him who is the Creator of hope. May our words and activities honor God as we seek His face in celebrating Black History Month.

We are gathered here today to celebrate Black History Month. God has richly blessed us with a heritage of His grace and mercy. May each of you be blessed as you observe and participate in the activities. May God be honored as we remember His love for all of us.

The beauty of the black experience in America is that "through it all, we learned to trust in Jesus." In the dark days of struggles and the bright days of blessing, God has been our strong arm. Thanks to each of you for coming to help us celebrate Black History Month.

Black History Month is a time for all Americans to observe the contributions and struggles of black people. Our history is deeply woven in the fabric of the American experience. Our hope is that this celebration will bring us closer together and strengthen areas of common familiarity. Dear God, please bless now our time together. Amen.

CONGRATULATIONS

Your hard and smart work has yielded a wonderful reward. On the occasion of your accomplishment, we congratulate you and wish you a bountiful future.

● ● ●

Colossians 3:23-24 says, "Whatever you do, work at it with all your heart, as working for the Lord, not for men, since you know that you will receive an inheritance from the Lord as a reward. It is the Lord Christ you are serving." Your wonderful work has been a testament to your love and dependence upon God. Congratulations, and God bless you for a job well done.

● ● ●

God gives gifts whereby we serve Him by serving others. Our work is often known only to God. But today, we congratulate you for completing your mission with diligence and excellence. May God grace your steps as you continue to serve Him.

● ● ●

Our hearts are swelling with pride over the great job you have accomplished. God has greatly gifted you to serve Him with excellence in all you do. We congratulate you for this great achievement and pray God's continued wisdom to you in the future.

● ● ●

Congratulations for a job done with excellence. Your teamwork and devotion was a thing of beauty to behold. May your continued efforts be blessed in your quest for excellence.

● ● ●

Thanks so much for what you have done for our company. May God continue to guide your steps in the pursuit of success. With a heart of gratitude, we congratulate you.

By now you are so used to being congratulated that it must be old hat to you. However, we never grow tired of congratulating you. Keep up the great work and again, congratulations!

EULOGIES

In times like these, words ring hollow in healing the pain of such a loss.

[Deceased] was a dear friend who loved God and [his/her] family. I personally knew [him/her] as a servant of God who was selfless and determined to make Christ known by [his/her] testimony.

I first met [name of deceased] in [time period]. We worked together as [jobs]. I grew to love and respect [him/her]. I have special memories of the time we [insert a specific story].

Earth is a better place because of the impact [name of deceased] had on our lives. Heaven is much brighter today because [he/she] is there. As a fitting tribute to [him/her], let us live for Christ as [he/she] did and make this world a much better place.

May God bless, comfort, and strengthen each of you.

Dear Lord, please give us grace to go on in the aftermath of the loss of [name of deceased]. [His/Her] life touched so many of us. As I eulogize this wonderful saint, give me the correct words to accurately express how I was touched by [his/her] life. Amen.

I first met [name of deceased] in [time period]. We worked together and served God in many ways: [name some church positions]. I know nothing of [him/her] except [he/she] was a person who loved God with all [his/her] heart. Was [he/she] perfect? Of course not, but [he/she] loved a perfect God who constantly made [him/her] more like Jesus. [His/Her] life was indeed a beautiful reflection of God's love.

The scriptures declare in Revelation 14:13, "Then I heard a voice from heaven say, 'Write: Blessed are the dead who die in the Lord from now on.' 'Yes,' says the Spirit, 'they will rest from their labor, for their deeds will follow them.'"

My dear friend is with the Lord. As a fitting memorial, let us emulate love for God and thereby join [him/her] in heaven when our journey is over. May God give you comfort and peace as you go forward from today's service.

The sadness of this day is made much easier because of what Jesus did on the cross for us. My lifelong friend [name of deceased] loved Jesus with all [his/her] heart and served Jesus with great distinction. Even though [he/she] is in heaven, we still miss [him/her].

While alive on earth, [he/she] did [his/her] best to care for family members and loved ones. [He/She] served faithfully at [name of church] as [positions in the church]. I was honored to call [him/her] a friend.

[His/Her] life was the epitome of Psalm 37:23, which says "The steps of a good man are ordered by the LORD: and he delighteth in his way." (KJV) This passage gives us not only a picture of [his/her] life but a road map for our lives. The greatest honor we could give to [him/her] is to love God like [he/she] did. Let us purpose to do that.

The heaviness of my heart is made lighter by the promise of eternal life through Jesus Christ. My dear friend believed in Jesus and is now in God's presence.

While with us, [he/she] did all [he/she] could to make Jesus known to others. [He/She] was an example of God's grace to [his/her] family, friends, and fellow employees. All of us are much richer because of the many ways [he/she] touched our lives. Heaven is a brighter place because [he/she] is there.

We honor people in various ways: Sometimes we erect statues in their memory, often, we rename bridges or streets in their name. However, the best way to honor [him/her] is to accept Jesus in your heart. This was [his/her] desire for all [he/she] met. Let us pray:

Dear God,

Thank You for sending salvation through Jesus Christ. Please comfort and strengthen us as we deal with the loss of our dear friend. Grant us the power to show God's love to all we meet, just as [he/she] did. Amen.

EULOGIES
FOR PETS

Pets are a source of comfort and support to many lonely people. The death of [name of pet] leaves an indelible hole in the hearts of all [he/she] loved. We thank God that [he/she] was a valuable part of our lives. May [owner's name] be comforted as [he/she] deals with this loss.

● ● ●

[Pet's name] was a faithful friend to [owner] for many years. [He/She] was there through the good times and the bad. This pet was a faithful friend who never complained. This death leaves us saddened yet thankful. For animals, just as for humans, "life is a vapor." May God bring comfort to all who will miss [pet's name].

● ● ●

We will sorely miss [pet's name]. [He/She] brought joy to our lives and love to our hearts. We should all try to live our lives for the good of others, as this pet did. We pray for [pet's owner] that God will comfort and strengthen [him/her].

● ● ●

The loss of a pet can be just as devastating as the loss of a close relative or friend. Pets bring love and acceptance to those they live with. We are here to remember [pet's name]. May God help us to so love one another.

● ● ●

We gather here in fond remembrance of [pet's name]. The love this pet brought to [owner's name] enhanced [his/her] emotional and physical health. As we thank God for this pet, let us also commit to live in a way to bless others.

HOMECOMING
WELCOME

We welcome you today to this homecoming service. What a delight to have you here. May our words and songs bring back memories of God's greatness in days gone by. So relax, enjoy yourself, and be blessed as we celebrate our homecoming service.

● ● ●

Earthly homecomings pale in comparison to our return when Christ comes to gather us home. Today we recall the blessings of God in this earthly place. May God rekindle the fervor for His Spirit as we celebrate your return to this humble place. Welcome and enjoy God in this place.

● ● ●

Homecoming service is a time for each of us to thank God for His blessings upon our past. We also renew past relationships and establish newer ones. God has blessed us today and we will sing His praises as we bless others. Join with us now as we commemorate the legacy of God's heritage in our midst.

● ● ●

We welcome each of you to this homecoming service. Whether you have come from far or near, you are equally welcomed. Join us now as we celebrate God's blessings in years past and His blessings today. God is worthy to be praised and we ask you to join with us in this homecoming celebration.

● ● ●

Homecoming is a time of returning to familiar places and seeing familiar faces. Our hope is that you will be renewed by the activities of this day. May the worship of the Savior refresh and replenish the spirit. We dedicate this time to God as we "turn our hearts towards home."

Someone once said, "Home is where the heart is." Well, our desire is that this homecoming service will allow each of us to experience community in a new way. May the words and music of this gathering facilitate joyful hearts and peaceful reflections. We welcome you all to join us as we experience a homecoming to remember.

● ● ●

We welcome you
   From near and far.
It doesn't matter
   Who you are.
Our homecoming prayer
   Is that you'll be
Blessed by God
   As you will see.

OFFERTORY COMMENTS

The scriptures tell us in Luke 6:38 to "Give, and it will be given to you. A good measure, pressed down, shaken together and running over, will be poured into your lap. For with the measure you use, it will be measured to you." Let us participate in the fulfillment of this verse by giving an offering to the Lord.

● ● ●

Now we have the opportunity to bless the Lord in a tangible way. By giving to God, we are not paying for blessing but giving to be a blessing. Everything we own is God's and we show His love by giving so that others may hear the gospel. Join with us now as we bless the Lord by our benevolence.

● ● ●

I want to thank each of you in advance for giving to the Lord. God has wonderfully blessed us with bountiful resources. We can now return a portion of His blessings so that others may hear God's Word. Dear Lord, please multiply this offering that it may facilitate the increase of the kingdom of God. Amen.

● ● ●

Heavenly Father, may our offering rise before You as a sweet sacrifice. We thank You that Jesus was sacrificed for us. His death brought us salvation, safety, and health. By godly wisdom, we gain the ability to make wealth. Bless us now as we give so that others may come to live for You. Amen.

● ● ●

Dear God, we thank You that we have this opportunity to give. We are happy to contribute to what You are doing in the earth. May these resources carry the gospel to those who have not heard. May they provide bread and sustenance to the hungry. Please bless each giver that they may be a partaker in Your blessings upon this earth. Again, we thank You. Amen.

One of the delights of Christianity is that of giving to the Lord in the form of an offering. An offering is over and above the tithe or ten percent. All the monies we give to God go far beyond our earthly travels. With our giving, missionaries are kept on the field, the hungry are fed and, most importantly, people hear God's Word. As we give, we emulate the nature of God, who gave His Son for us. Let us give now to the glory of God and to the benefit of others.

RETIREMENT CEREMONIES

Retirement is not a time for sitting on one's laurels. It is a time of transition. [Name] has faithfully served as [job titles] and is now ready to move on to other pursuits. We bid [him/her] Godspeed and wish [him/her] well as [he/she] makes this transition.

● ● ●

Our prayers and best wishes go forth on behalf of [name] as [he/she] retires. Of course, we all know that [he/she] will not languish away in some rocking chair or waste time playing shuffleboard. [His/Her] faithful service to [company] set the standard for diligence and competence. May [his/her] future be bright as [he/she] moves on to serve in other arenas.

● ● ●

Retirement is more than a time of reflection. It is a time of projection. People don't stop living when they retire. They often transition to more productive activities. [Name] is still full of life and should handle retirement very well. Our best wishes go with [him/her] as [he/she] "re-fires" instead of retires.

● ● ●

[Name], today is your day. You have been working here for over [number of years]. We pray you will have a wonderful day off before you go on to your next job. Seriously, you have served faithfully and we pray God's best to you in the coming days.

● ● ●

We pray God's continued blessings to [name] as [he/she] moves into retirement. [He/She] has faithfully served this company. [His/Her] example of excellence and diligence shall long be emulated. We wish [him/her] well.

Retirement is a time of transition. For [name] it will probably be a move from this job to even harder work. The only thing [he/she] doesn't do well is nothing. We wish [him/her] well as [he/she] moves on to the next chapter of [his/her] life. May God richly bless [him/her] as [he/she] moves on.

We bid [name] the very best as [he/she] begins retirement. [He/She] served for [number of years] as [job titles]. Now [he/she] moves to the most exciting phase of [his/her] life. May God bless and energize [name] as [he/she] continues [his/her] service to mankind.

SCHOLARSHIP PRESENTATIONS

The finalists for the [name of scholarship] are [names of students]. Each of these scholars has labored with diligent wisdom. Their deeds serve as a benchmark for future applicants. With great delight, I present the [name of scholarship] to [names of winners].

● ● ●

Scholarship winners are students of academics who will always be students of life. We are very proud of this group of applicants. They are ready to enter the next phase of their pursuits. May each of them use this opportunity to better themselves and to help mankind. With great delight, I present to you, [names of winners], the [name of scholarship].

● ● ●

A scholarship can be a ticket to life's next level. It's our hope that each of our winners will use this ticket to prepare themselves to make the world a better place. We pray that they will continue to pave the path of excellence for future generations. Let's now recognize our [name of scholarship] winners: [names of winners].

● ● ●

We thank God for each of our scholarship winners. Their quest for excellence is both admirable and enviable. Many competed, but today we recognize the winners in this strenuous contest. Ladies and gentlemen, the winners of the [name of scholarship] are [name of winners]. Let's give them a hand!

● ● ●

The [name of scholarship] committee thanks each person who applied. Each application reflected hard work and academic brilliance. This year's winners are as follows: [names of winners].

We are thankful for each student who competed in this scholarship competition. Their tireless study and labor is an example of excellence to each of us. May God continue to bless them with their quest for superior accomplishment. I now present to you the winners of the [name of scholarship]. They are as follows: [names of winners].

Our scholarship committee had a hard time determining winners of this year's scholarship. Virtually all of the students were brilliant students with a bright future. We sincerely thank each person who applied and wish them the best. This year's winners of the [name of scholarship] are: [names of winners].

HANGING OF THE GREENS
Service 1

LEADER: Greetings and welcome to each of you. We are here today to celebrate the coming of the Savior!

ALL: Grace and peace to you and to all for whom He came.

LEADER: May the Prince of Peace be the King of our lives. May His name be proclaimed from the shopping malls to the classroom hallways. Join us now as we read from God's Holy Word:

Isaiah 9:6-7 [NIV]

LEADER: "For to us a child is born, to us a son is given, and the government will be on his shoulders. And he will be called . . .

ALL: "Wonderful Counselor, Mighty God, Everlasting Father, Prince of Peace.

LEADER: "Of the increase of his government and peace there will be no end. He will reign on David's throne and over his kingdom, establishing and upholding it with justice and righteousness from that time on and forever. The zeal of the Lord Almighty will accomplish this."

LEADER: May God add a blessing to the reading of His Word.

Lighting of the Advent Candle

LEADER: Today we rejoice that this wonderful prophecy was fulfilled in millennia past. We also rejoice in the Advent of the Baby who became the propitiation or atoning sacrifice for our sins. The Psalm writer declared in Psalm 90:2 that, "Before the mountains were born or you brought forth the earth and the world, from everlasting to everlasting you are God."

(The LEADER *picks up the Advent wreath and displays it as he/she continues.)*
This circular evergreen wreath represents the unending, everlasting hope we have in Christ. We rejoice in the hope of Christ's return. Three of the four candles are purple, the color of royalty, and represent repentance in preparation

105

for Christ's second Advent. The center candle is white and will be lit upon the return of Christ. In the song *Have Yourself a Merry Little Christmas*, the words say, ". . . everybody knows some holly and some mistletoe helps to make the season bright . . ." The significance of these two elements not only makes the season bright but also brightens our lives. The holly represents the crown of the crucified Christ. Some theologians tell us the yellow berries became crimson when Christ's blood was shed on Mount Calvary. The mistletoe represents Christ's everlasting love. Most people today would equate the mistletoe with being kissed by a special person. However, centuries before Jesus came, Jeremiah 31:3 declared of God, "I have loved you with an everlasting love; I have drawn you with loving-kindness." No kiss under the mistletoe can compare to the divine kiss by Christ to the Church, one day soon.

Suggested Song: *Jesus, Name Above All Names*

Hanging the Greens

LEADER: The psalmist writes: "Blessed is he who comes in the name of the LORD."

    The town of Bethlehem was not ready for the first coming of Christ. Instead of a clean hospital room, the Savior was born in a cave. However, we rejoice at His Advent [coming] and by faith we prepare for His second coming as our hearts shout, "Hosanna!"

    Many of us will celebrate the arrival of relatives and loved-ones for the holidays. Grandparents will revel at the arrival of children and grandchildren. Many parents recall the days of their youth as their bright-eyed children partake of bountiful food and open their presents. However, with all of our earthly blessings, the appreciation of our heavenly blessing remains foremost in our hearts.

Prayer of Thanks

LEADER: Dear God, Adam's loss in the garden was reclaimed by the Baby in the manger. Mere human words cannot express appreciation for the price Christ paid for our sins. Grant us please the grace to live by the Spirit's power and show in tangible ways our thanks to Jesus. Help us to walk as a living sermon seen by all men. Help us to show our appreciation by being "the one beggar who showed the other beggar where he found bread." Thank you, Lord, that we can be part of the "divine romance" of love given to us by Jesus. Amen.

Suggested Song: *Emmanuel*

Evergreen Placement

LEADER: The greenery of the season is missing during the Christmas season. In the fall, the crackle of leaves creates a symphony as we walk in the late afternoon. Raking leaves provides an excellent opportunity for young children to make extra money in preparation for Thanksgiving and Christmas. During the Christmas season, the dryness of the fall season is countered by the sweet smell of evergreen and the freshness of this plant.

Centuries ago, Mary and Joseph trekked through some rough terrain en route to pay taxes in the city of David. Little did the Bethlehem Chamber of Commerce know that the Messiah would be born in its city limits. The people of Bethlehem went from place to place unaware of history's greatest moment. Tired and worn out, Joseph and Mary strode into town to do their civic duty. Today they could have mailed a check or filed by e-mail, but for them such luxury was not to be. They were players in a drama, which culminated in "the fullness of time." Their lot was not to be that of the rich and famous. Yet the precious treasure of her womb would grow up to change the landscape of history. Little did Mary and Joseph know that they would have to escape to save the life of the Baby. Herod's murderous rage caused by his jealousy drove Joseph and Mary out of town. Through it all, God guided their steps to safer places.

Tradition says that during their escape, Joseph, Mary, and Jesus were shielded from the soldiers by the cedar leaves on a nearby hillside. This symbol of eternal promise and everlasting life was epitomized by Jesus' death and resurrection on the cross some thirty years later. Please rise as we sing *Nothing But the Blood of Jesus*.

Suggested Song: *Nothing But the Blood of Jesus*

The Legend of the Christmas Tree

LEADER: Good Christians differ on the issue of whether or not to have a Christmas tree in their homes. While both have legitimate views on the history of this tradition, the fact remains that the Christmas tree is a key symbol of this season. The reputed founder of the Protestant movement, Martin Luther, is said to have adorned and lighted one of the first Christmas trees. Since then, families around the world have gathered to place ornaments on Christmas trees and to place presents under the tree. These presents are, in a sense, a type of God's present to us in His Son, Jesus. In reality, Jesus is "the gift that keeps on giving." As we receive His gift of eternal life, we too continue to give to others from "the well that never runs dry."

Suggested Song: *O Christmas Tree*

The Poinsettia Story

LEADER: During the 1820s, Joel Roberts Poinsett served as United States Ambassador to Mexico. Ambassador Poinsett was also an amateur botanist who grew to love the *Euphorbia pulcherrima*, the botanical name given the plant by a German botanist. Poinsett was particularly touched by the story of how the plant became part of religious lore. Several stories abound concerning the religious significance of the plant; but one of two Mexican children taking the plant to a nativity service remains prominent.

Apparently, the brother and sister had no gift to take to the nativity service. They both made a bouquet of weeds for their gift. While the other children laughed at them, God saw the sincerity of their hearts and according to legend, their weeds became a beautiful flower which we now know as the poinsettia. Then, just as now, "man looks at the outward appearance; but God looks at the heart." Upon his re-

108

turn to America, Ambassador Poinsett introduced the plant to his native South Carolina and it has become an American favorite over the past two centuries. They can be procured in colors of red—the most preferred color—white or pink. During this season, let us be thankful for this beautiful plant which has grown to symbolize the beauty of Christmas and the vibrancy of life.

Suggested Song: *O Come, Let Us Adore Him*

Offering Prayer

LEADER: Dear God, we thank You for sending Jesus. He came to give His life for each of us. Now as we give of our earthly treasure, take our offering and make it a beautiful flower, just as legend said You did with the poinsettia plant. Please bless now each giver and each receiver of our gifts to You. Amen!

Congregational Prayer

LEADER: Dear God, as one part of Your body around the earth, we thank You for sending Jesus. Grant to each of us the ability to reflect His love to everyone we know. Grace us to walk as He walked in the power of the Spirit. Live through each of us in a way that honors the Child in the manger and reveres the Spirit of this wonderful season. We pray these blessings in the name of Jesus. Amen

Suggested Song: *The Lord's Prayer*

Benediction

LEADER: May God's love and the Spirit of Christ envelop and protect you as you go from this place. May Christmas be a perennial time of reflection and reverence of the Child in the manger and the risen Christ. May each of you be an ambassador of God's abiding love in your hearts. Go now in peace, hope, and the expectation of great blessings from God and to humanity.

HANGING OF THE GREENS

SERVICE 2

(Urban Rendition)

Cast:

> BOBBY
> JAMAAL
> PASTOR SMITH

Production Notes: Bobby and Jamaal are walking into the church. A few minutes later, they are joined by Pastor Smith. They walk through the hanging of the greens as the audience observes their interaction.

BOBBY: Pastor Smith said he wants us to be part of a service called "hanging the greens."

JAMAAL: Why do we want to hang the Greens? They are such a nice family. Besides, when I told my Dad what he said, he thought it had something to do with collard greens.

BOBBY: I don't think he was talking about the Green family or collard greens, but some type of Christmas ceremony. You know Pastor Smith; he is always coming up with new ideas.

JAMAAL: Yeah, remember last year when he rode his motorcycle into the church . . . my grandmother dropped her false teeth onto the floor.

BOBBY: Yeah, I will never forget that . . .

PASTOR SMITH: Hello, boys. Are you ready to practice for the Christmas service?

JAMAAL: Well, Pastor, I think I am . . . what kind of surprises will you have for us this year?

PASTOR SMITH: Jamaal, I promise not to ride my bike into the service again. I hope your grandmother recovered from that little incident last year.

JAMAAL: She is OK, but she will never forget how you rode in dressed as Santa Claus. She said you are the only preacher she knows who rides a motorcycle. Most of the pastors she knew drove Cadillacs.

PASTOR SMITH (*laughing*): Well, I thought about that but I don't own a Cadillac.

(*As they approach the altar area, all three laugh heartily at* PASTOR'S *joke.*)

PASTOR SMITH: Hey, guys, hanging the greens is a Christmas tradition. In this ceremony, we recognize the beauty and elegance that is uniquely Christmas.

BOBBY: You mean the presents, Christmas trees, the toys . . .?

PASTOR SMITH (*smiling*): Well, Bobby, those things do remind us of Christmas but the reality of Christmas is presence spelled p-r-e-s-e-n-c-e. By that I mean the presence of the Christ-child, Jesus.

(PASTOR SMITH *picks up his Bible and turns to Luke 2.*)

JAMAAL: Pastor Smith, is Christmas in the Bible?

PASTOR SMITH: Well, Jamaal, let's read about the story of Christmas. In Luke 2, the Bible reads, "In those days Caesar Augustus issued a decree that a census should be taken of the entire Roman world. [This was the first census that took place while Quirinius was governor of Syria.] And everyone went to his own town to register. So Joseph also went up from the town of Nazareth in Galilee to Judea, to Bethlehem the town of David, because he belonged to the house and line of David. He went there to register with Mary, who was pledged to be married to him and was expecting a child."

(*After reading verses 1-5,* PASTOR SMITH *looks up at the boys.*)

PASTOR SMITH: You see, boys, Joseph and Mary went to Bethlehem to register for the census or counting of people. The time of the census coincided with the birth of Jesus. Many would say it was a coincidence but actually it was the result of prophecy or God's Word coming to pass. Jamaal, you want to read a few verses starting at verse 6?

(PASTOR SMITH *hands his Bible to* JAMAAL.)

JAMAAL: Yes, Pastor. (*Reading*) "While they were there, the time came for the baby to be born, and she gave birth to her firstborn, a son. She wrapped him in cloths and placed him in a manger, because there was no room for them in the inn. And there were shepherds living out in the fields nearby, keeping watch over their flocks at night. An angel of the Lord appeared to them, and the glory of the Lord shone around them, and they were terrified. But the angel said to them, 'Do not be afraid. I bring you good news of great joy that will be for all the people. Today in the town of David a Savior has been born to you; he is Christ the Lord. This will be a sign to you: You will find a baby wrapped in cloths and lying in a manger.'"

(JAMAAL *stops reading and looks at* PASTOR SMITH.)

JAMAAL: Pastor, why didn't Joseph and Mary go to the hospital? By the way, what is a manger? And those angels . . . were those guardian angels?

PASTOR SMITH (*smiling*): Jamaal, they did not have hospitals like we do today. A manger, well it is a box that holds food for animals. The angels . . . well, you could consider them guardian angels. By the way, the stable in which Jesus was born was in all probability a cave . . .

BOBBY: Pastor, may I read?

PASTOR SMITH: I am sorry, Bobby. Please excuse me for talking so much. Please read from verses 13 to 20.

Suggested Song: *Away in a Manger*

BOBBY (*reading*): "Suddenly a great company of the heavenly host appeared with the angel, praising God and saying, 'Glory to God in the highest, and on earth peace to men on whom his favor rests.' When the angels had left them and gone into heaven, the shepherds said to one another, 'Let's go to Bethlehem and see this thing that has happened, which the Lord has told us about.' So they hurried off and found Mary and Joseph, and the baby, who was lying in the manger. When they had seen him, they spread the word concerning what had been told them about this child, and all who heard it were amazed at what the shepherds said to them. But Mary treasured up all these things and pondered them in her heart. The shepherds returned, glorifying and praising God for all the things they had heard and seen, which were just as they had been told."

JAMAAL: Wow! That is quite a story!

PASTOR SMITH: That's history's greatest love story. You see, the presents, the Christmas trees, and the toys pale in comparison to the real reason why Jesus came to earth.

BOBBY: Pastor, why did He come?

PASTOR SMITH: Jesus came as a child, grew to be a man, and died on the cross for our sins. You see, the Christmas story points to the Easter story. But for now, let's stick with the Christmas story.

BOBBY: What about hanging the greens?

JAMAAL: Yeah, I could use some greens myself.

PASTOR SMITH: OK, boys, let's look at some of the commonly known elements of the season. For example, where does the Christmas tree come from?

JAMAAL: Well, we get our Christmas tree from the lot on the corner.

PASTOR SMITH *(laughing and pointing to the various elements as he talks)*: Jamaal, I meant where does the tradition come from. Also, why do we include evergreens in the Christmas tradition? What about these beautiful poinsettia plants?

Suggested Song: *O Christmas Tree*

PASTOR SMITH: Jamaal, what do you think is the most common symbol of Christmas?

JAMAAL: At my house, it is the Christmas tree. What about your house, Bobby?

BOBBY: Well, it is probably a toss-up between the Christmas tree and Santa Claus . . . and don't forget those presents.

PASTOR SMITH (*walking over to the Christmas tree*): Tradition has it that Martin Luther . . .

JAMAAL (*interrupting*): You mean Dr. Martin Luther King?

PASTOR SMITH: Well, good guess, but long before Dr. King's birth, his namesake, a priest named Martin Luther, started the tradition of Christmas tree decoration. He placed a star on top of the tree symbolizing the star referred to in Matthew 2:2 when the Magi said, "Where is the one who has been born king of the Jews? We saw his star in the east and have come to worship him." Martin Luther also placed candles on the tree representing the splendor of the heavens above. Psalm 19:1 states, "The heavens declare the glory of God; the skies proclaim the work of his hands." Martin Luther recognized the awesomeness of God's creation.

BOBBY (*picking up a piece of holly and ivy*): Pastor, what is the importance of the evergreen in the Christmas tradition?

PASTOR SMITH: Bobby, evergreens represent "the unchanging nature of God." Some writers believe it symbolizes joy, peace, and victory. Early Christians decorated their homes with evergreens as a picture of Christ's abiding presence.

JAMAAL: When they put evergreens up in their homes, did they call it "hanging the greens?"

PASTOR SMITH: You know, they just may have.

JAMAAL: What about these red plants? Poinsett plants?

PASTOR SMITH: Well, they are actually called poinsettia plants. They were named after the first United States Ambassador to Mexico, Joel Roberts Poinsett. He served as our ambassador in the 1820s. He is known for bringing the poinsettia plant to America. In Mexico, it was sometimes known as the "Flower of the Holy Night." The red star-shaped petals remind us of the star that led the wise men to the Messiah's manger. In some sense, as the light of our lives shines, it can lead others to the risen Messiah.

BOBBY: You know, Christmas is a lot more than just toys and trees and stuff.

PASTOR SMITH: Yes, Bobby, it is. (*Motions for both boys to join him and sit down near the Christmas tree.*) Christmas reminds us of a time in the Garden of Eden before sin existed. The story is told in Genesis chapters one through five. Adam and Eve were placed in a place of perfection. They walked with God and had no need to fear any animal in the garden. They could eat of any tree in the garden except the tree of the knowledge of good and evil. Then it happened . . .

JAMAAL: What happened?

PASTOR SMITH: Adam and Eve sinned against God by obeying the serpent [Lucifer] and eating of the forbidden tree. As a result, sin infected every person born after Adam because of Adam's sin.

JAMAAL: That's not fair!

PASTOR SMITH: Jamaal, it does not sound fair but it happened. You see, everyone born after Adam needed a Savior. God told Adam that the "seed of the woman" or descendant of Eve, would bruise the head of the serpent.

This was one of the first references to the coming of Jesus. Until Jesus came, untold numbers of animals were sacrificed but their blood only covered man's sin. At Christmas, we celebrate the birth of the Christ child. He came, lived a sinless life, and became the sacrifice for our sins. His blood washes away the sins of anyone who by faith receives Him. In other words, when someone believes in Jesus, he is born again. That is why Jesus was born and why we celebrate His birth at Christmas.

BOBBY: Pastor that is definitely the greatest story ever told!

Suggested Song: *Nothing But the Blood of Jesus*

PASTOR SMITH: Ladies and gentlemen, thanks for attending our hanging the greens program today. Our prayer is that the Child of Christmas becomes the Lord of your lives. Let us pray: Dear God, thanks for sending Jesus. May the symbols of Christmas remind us of His sacrificial love and continuing grace. Help us to show forth Your love in all we do, feel, say, and think. Amen.